IT'S ELECTRIC!

ELECTRIC CARS

Jessica Rusick

Big Buddy Books

An Imprint of Abdo Publishing

abdobooks.com

abdobooks.com

Published by Abdo Publishing, a division of ABDO, PO Box 398166, Minneapolis, Minnesota 55439.

Printed in the United States of America, North Mankato, Minnesota
052023
092023

THIS BOOK CONTAINS RECYCLED MATERIALS

Design: Sarah DeYoung, Mighty Media, Inc.
Production: Mighty Media, Inc.
Editor: Katherine Chu
Cover Photograph: Mike Mareen/Shutterstock Images
Interior Photographs: hapabapa/iStockphoto, p. 21; Jarlat Maletych/Shutterstock Images, p. 5; joel-t/iStockphoto, p. 11; Mike Mareen/Shutterstock Images, pp. 23, 24–25, 29 (Lucid Air); nomis_h/Shutterstock Images, p. 15; RoschetzkyIstockPhoto/iStockphoto, pp. 18–19, 29 (Tesla Model 3); sylv1rob1/Shutterstock Images, p. 17; Tramino/iStockphoto, pp. 9, 13, 28 (Tesla Roadster, Nissan Leaf); VanderWolf Images/Shutterstock Images, p. 27; Ziga Plahutar/iStockphoto, p. 7
Design Elements: octopusaga/Shutterstock Images (hexagon pattern); Vlad Malinovskij/Shutterstock Images (lightning bolt icon); Zoa.Arts/Shutterstock Images (lightning)

Library of Congress Control Number: 2022948827

Publisher's Cataloging-in-Publication Data
Names: Rusick, Jessica, author.
Title: Electric cars / by Jessica Rusick
Description: Minneapolis, Minnesota : Abdo Publishing, 2024 | Series: It's electric! | Includes online resources and index.
Identifiers: ISBN 9781098291549 (lib. bdg.) | ISBN 9781098278007 (ebook)
Subjects: LCSH: Electric automobiles--Juvenile literature. | Cars (Automobiles)--Juvenile literature. | Electric vehicles--Juvenile literature. | Transportation--Juvenile literature.
Classification: DDC 388--dc23

CONTENTS

CHAPTER 1

SPEED & STEALTH

A sleek car waits at a stoplight. The light turns green. Zoom! The car zips down the road. It quickly reaches 60 miles per hour (97 kmh). But this car makes almost no noise! That's because it's an electric **vehicle** (EV).

FAST FACT

Electric cars were invented in the 1800s. They were popular in the early 1900s before gas-powered cars became more affordable.

In 2022, the Rimac Nevera was the fastest EV in the world. Its top speed was 256 miles per hour (412 kmh)!

CHAPTER 2

WHY ELECTRIC?

An EV's **motor** is powered by electricity. The electricity is stored in **rechargeable batteries**. Since the early 2000s, electric cars have exploded in popularity for a number of reasons.

Gas cars **release** gases that harm Earth. Electric cars do not. Charging an electric car costs less than buying gas. Electric cars can also be easier to take care of.

An electric car can be recharged by plugging it into an outlet or special charger.

CHAPTER 3

INSPIRING START

In 2008, car company Tesla **Motors released** the Roadster electric sports car. A new type of **lithium-ion battery** made it fast and powerful. Tesla built 2,400 Roadsters between 2008 and 2012.

FAST FACT

By 2022, most electric cars used lithium-ion batteries.

When it was released, the Tesla Roadster cost $110,000. It could drive 245 miles (394 km) on one charge.

CHAPTER 4

NISSAN LEAF

Other car companies had also started to create EVs. In 2010, Nissan began selling its electric car, the Leaf. It was the first widely **available** electric car.

Drivers liked the Leaf's **affordable** price of $32,500. But the car could only drive 100 miles (161 km) on one charge.

The Nissan Leaf's charging port is on the hood. Its batteries are under the floor.

Nissan improved its **lithium-ion batteries** to increase the Leaf's driving range. In 2022, the Leaf had a range of 149 miles (240 km). Its top speed was 90 miles per hour (145 kmh). And it could be charged up to 80 percent in 40 minutes. The Leaf remained popular and **affordable**. By 2022, Nissan had sold 500,000 Leafs worldwide!

Nissan Leafs are designed to cut through the air as they move. This helps the cars travel faster and gives them a longer range!

CHAPTER 5

TESLA MODEL 3

Since **releasing** the Roadster in 2008, Tesla had become known for **expensive**, **high-quality** electric cars. In 2016, Tesla released its **design** for a new car called the Tesla Model 3.

Tesla had worked with **researchers** to improve its **lithium-ion battery**. The battery could store more energy. It also cost less to make. This meant Tesla could sell its new car at a lower price!

More than 230,000 people pre-ordered the Model 3 in the two days after its design was released in 2016.

The first Model 3 became **available** in 2017. The car was fast. And it could drive up to 310 miles (499 km) on one charge!

Buyers thought the Model 3 was **high-quality** yet **affordable**. By 2022, it was the best-selling electric car of all time. By 2023, more than 1 million had been sold!

The Tesla Model 3's interior had a simple design. It featured a large touchscreen and few buttons.

TESLA MODEL 3

Starting price: $40,390

Top speed: 140 miles per hour (225 kmh)

Range: 267 to 272 miles (430 to 438 km) on one charge

Acceleration: 0 to 60 miles per hour (97 kmh) in 5.8 seconds

Charging time: 15 minutes to charge up to 175 miles (282 km)

Statistics from 2023 model with Rear-Wheel Drive

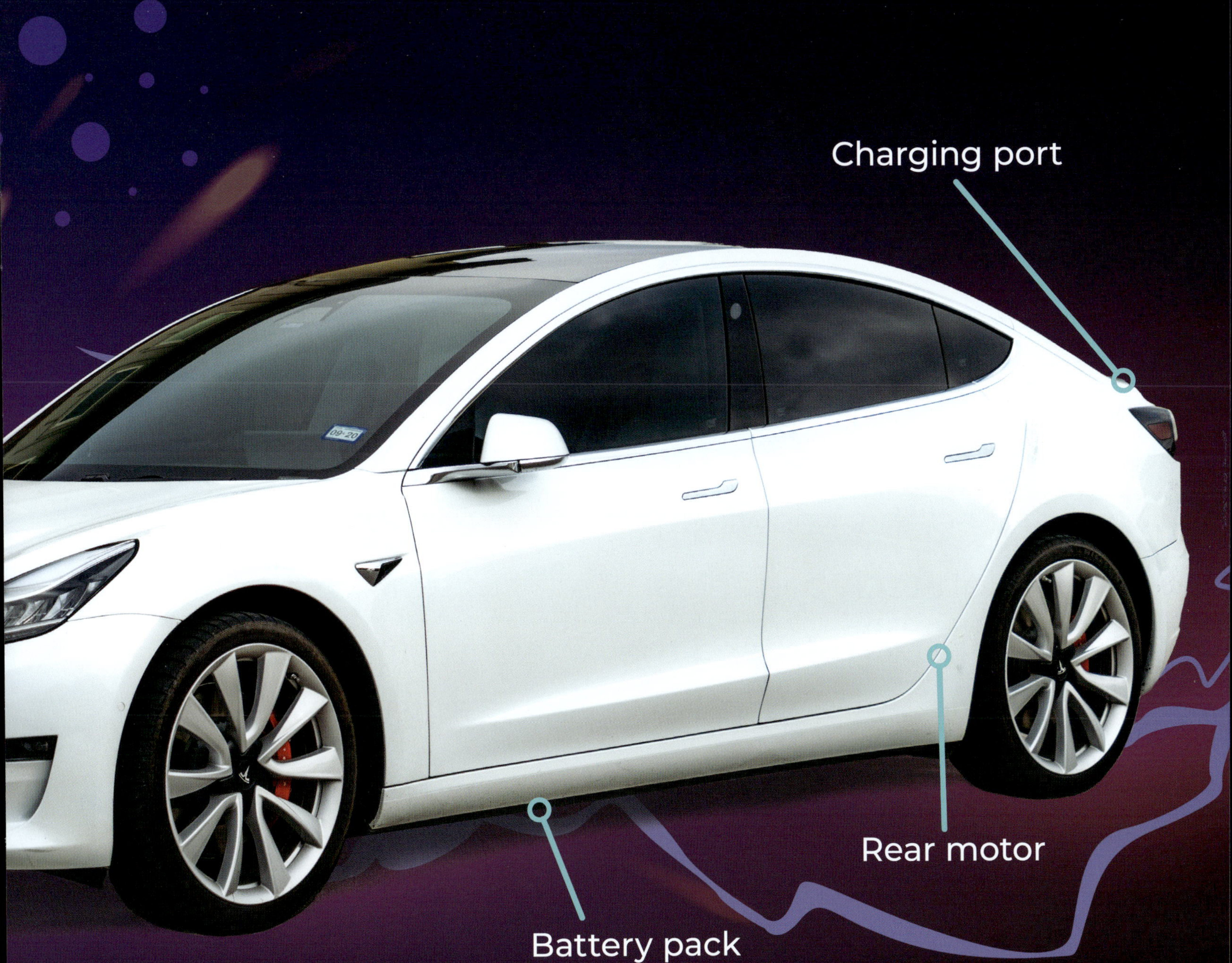
Charging port
Rear motor
Battery pack

CHAPTER 6

LUCID AIR

Lucid **Motors** was founded in 2007. At first, it made **batteries** for other EVs. Lucid used this knowledge to create its own high-tech batteries.

Lucid **released** the Air electric car in 2021. It was one of the most powerful electric cars for sale!

By 2023, Lucid had released five different Air models. They were the Sapphire, Pure, Touring, Grand Touring, and Dream Edition.

The Dream Edition was the first Air model to be **released**. It had a range of 520 miles (837 km)! This was the longest range of any EV on the market. Buyers were happy with the car's power. They also loved its quick and easy **steering**, sleek **design**, and fast charge time.

The Lucid Air's design was loosely based on the shape of an aircraft.

LUCID AIR

Starting price: $170,650

Top speed: 173 miles per hour (278 kmh)

Range: 520 miles (837 km) on one charge

Acceleration: 0 to 60 miles per hour (97 kmh) in 2.6 seconds

Charging time: 21 minutes to charge up to 300 miles (483 km)

Statistics from 2022 Dream Edition

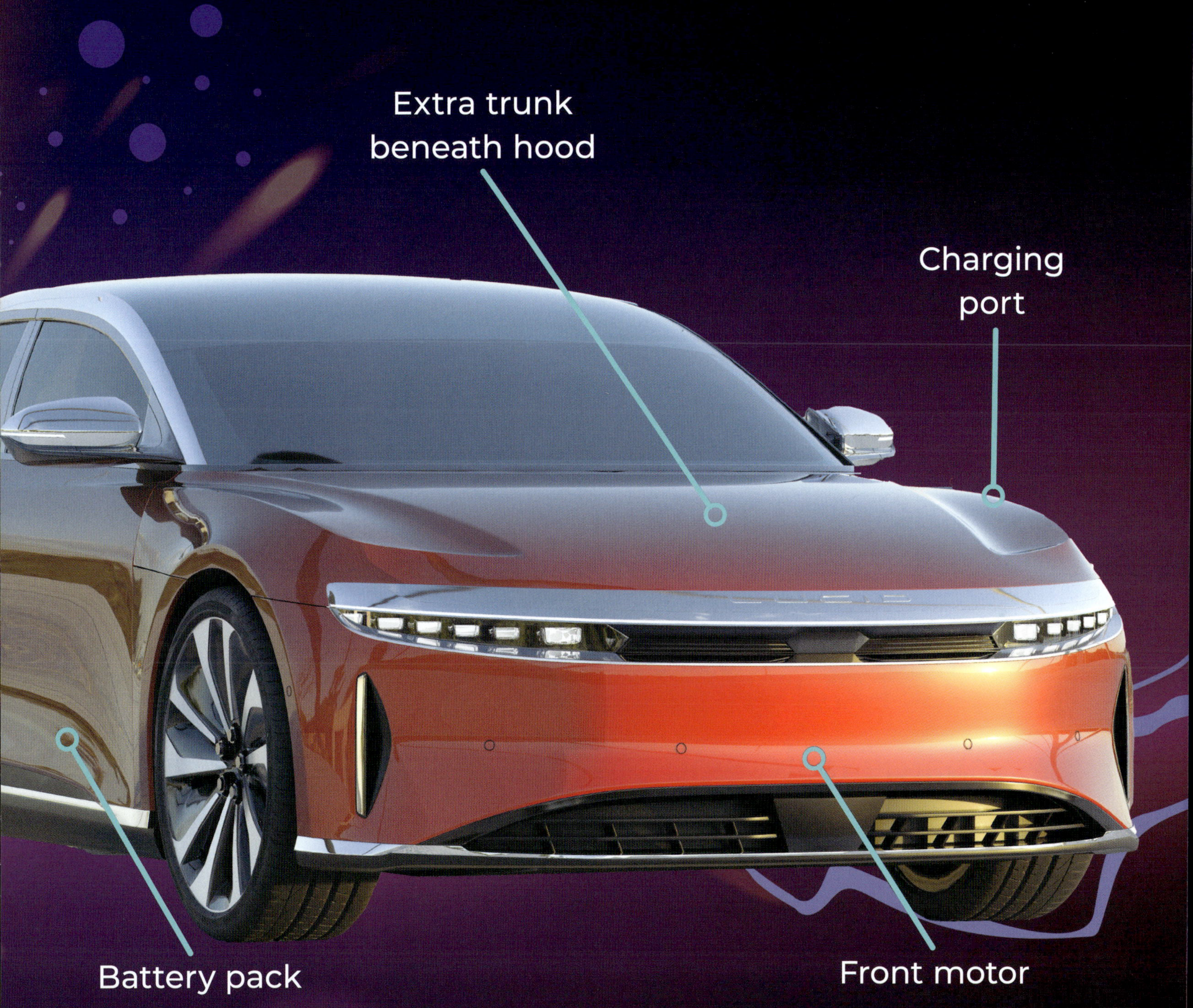
Extra trunk beneath hood
Charging port
Battery pack
Front motor

CHAPTER 7

THE FUTURE'S ELECTRIC

Most major car companies plan to **release** new electric cars in the coming years. And new companies continue to enter the EV market. Meanwhile, **researchers** are improving EV **batteries**. They hope to make electric cars that can charge faster and cost less. In the **future**, electric cars could rule the road!

Major car company Ford said it will stop making gas-powered cars by 2040. In 2021, it debuted the Ford Mustang Mach-E, an electric SUV.

TIMELINE

2007

Lucid **Motors** is founded. The company makes **batteries** for EVs.

2010

Nissan begins selling the Leaf. It is the first widely **available** electric car.

2008

The Tesla Roadster is **released**.

2016

Tesla **releases** the **design** for the Model 3.

2021

The Lucid Air is released. It has the longest range of any electric car on the market.

2017

The Tesla Model 3 is made **available**. It later becomes the best-selling electric car of all time.

GLOSSARY

affordable—having a cost that is not too high.

available—able to be had or used.

battery—a small container filled with chemicals that makes electrical power.

design (dih-ZINE)—a plan for how something will appear or work.

expensive—having a high price.

future (FYOO-chuhr)—a time that has not yet occurred.

high-quality—very good or excellent.

lithium-ion battery—a rechargeable battery that uses lithium ions as the primary component.

motor—a machine that produces motion or power for doing work.

recharge—to become charged again. Rechargeable means that something is able to be charged again.

release—to let go or make available to the public.

researcher—a person who carefully studies a subject in order to learn facts about it.

steering—relating to guiding or controlling a moving vehicle.

vehicle—something used for carrying persons or large objects. Some examples of vehicles are cars, trucks, boats, and airplanes.

ONLINE RESOURCES

Booklinks
NONFICTION NETWORK
FREE! ONLINE NONFICTION RESOURCES

To learn more about electric cars, visit abdobooklinks.com. These links are routinely monitored and updated to provide the most current information available.

INDEX